Machine Learning for Disease Identification in Oil Palm Leaves

Hamdani
Anindita Septiarini
Emy Setyaningsih

Acknowledgments

We would like to express our heartfelt gratitude to the individuals and organizations who have contributed to the realization of this book, "Machine Learning for Disease Identification in Oil Palm Leaves".

Our Profound Thanks to:

- Our families, for their support and understanding during the long hours and late nights dedicated to this project.

- The research community, for their valuable insights, collaboration, and shared knowledge that have enriched the content of this book.

- Our colleagues and peers in the field of computer systems and technology at the Department of Informatics, Faculty of Engineering, Universitas Mulawarman, East Kalimantan, and Department of Computer Systems Engineering, Faculty of Information Technology and Business, Institut Sains & Technology AKPRIND Yogyakarta, for their encouragement and inspiration.

- The reviewers and experts who provided critical feedback and suggestions to enhance the quality and rigor of our work.

- The entire team at the publishing house who worked diligently to bring this book to life and make it accessible to a broader audience.

This book would not have been possible without the collective effort and support of everyone mentioned above. We are truly thankful for your contributions to our work.

Sincerely,

Hamdani and Anindita Septiarini
Department of Informatics, Faculty of Engineering, Universitas Mulawarman, East Kalimantan, Indonesia

Emy Setyaningsih
Department of Computer Systems Engineering, Faculty of Information Technology and Business, Institut Sains & Technology AKPRIND Yogyakarta, Indonesia

Table of Contents

CHAPTER 1 | INTRODUCTION

1.1 Background

Palm oil holds a significant position in Indonesia's economy, serving as a vital source of non-oil and gas foreign exchange. Indonesia stands as one of the world's largest palm oil producers, with the East Kalimantan region being a prominent contributor to this production. The versatile nature of palm oil makes it a crucial component in the daily diets of over three billion individuals (Murphy et al., 2021). Moreover, it can be processed into crude oil and renewable fuels, making oil palm a pivotal crop for both food and non-food industries.

The palm oil industry plays a pivotal role in the global economy, as it stands as a major source of vegetable oil. It accounts for approximately 40% of all globally traded vegetable oil (Murphy et al., 2021). Nevertheless, the 2020s have brought about substantial challenges to oil palm production, particularly in terms of plant health, spanning from seedling to harvest. The industry grapples with the growing incidence of pests and diseases affecting various parts of the oil palm trees, including the roots, leaves, fruits, and trunks. This challenge, coupled with climate-related issues like rising temperatures and unpredictable rainfall patterns, significantly impacts the quality and quantity of oil palm production in Indonesia

(Santoso et al., 2017). As a result, oil palm health becomes a critical consideration for optimizing production, both for companies and individual plantation owners.

Diseases in oil palm predominantly manifest on the leaves, with yellow leaf spot being a common affliction. As noted by Pornsuriya et al. (2013), initial symptoms include small spots appearing in the inner circle of young leaves, which then expand into larger yellow spots. These yellow spots, characterized by elongation and the presence of brown spots at their centers, can affect leaves at various stages of growth (Kovachich, 1956). Detecting leaf diseases can be based on these visible characteristics.

While manual detection by humans based on visual leaf patterns is feasible, it lacks effectiveness, especially in large-scale applications. Psychological factors like fatigue or health conditions may lead to inaccuracies. Laboratory testing is an option but proves time-consuming and costly, particularly for farmers. Additionally, the limited knowledge about disease symptoms among farmers, communities, and plantation managers often results in misdiagnosis, delaying disease management efforts (Ji et al., 2020). Hence, conventional methods relying on visual observation have limitations concerning accuracy and timeliness, which can impede the containment of diseases.

In recent years, the emergence of artificial intelligence and digital image processing technologies has transformed various sectors, including agriculture and plantations. Machine learning, a subset of artificial intelligence, shows promise in enhancing the accuracy and response time of plant disease detection solutions.

Digital image processing can aid in recognizing intricate disease patterns on oil palm leaves that may elude human perception. Incorporating machine learning can lead to swifter and more precise identification of oil palm conditions, facilitating more effective countermeasures.

1.2   The Purpose of The Book

The significance of a monograph book titled "Machine Learning for Disease Identification in Oil Palm Leaves" is underscored by the background information provided. This book serves as a comprehensive exploration of the utilization of machine learning technology in the precise identification of diseases in oil palm leaves, encompassing images with diverse and intricate backgrounds.

The book delves into the intricacies of this method, elucidating how it operates in the automated differentiation of healthy and diseased oil palm plants based on their leaves. The process of identifying leaf diseases in oil palm plants, meticulously detailed within these pages, encompasses several pivotal stages. These include the detection of Regions of Interest (RoI), essential pre-processing steps, feature extraction, judicious feature selection, and classification techniques. In essence, this monograph fills a critical knowledge gap, offering a deep dive into the innovative world of machine learning for disease detection in oil palm leaves. It stands as an indispensable resource for researchers, practitioners, and enthusiasts in the field, providing invaluable insights into cutting-edge technology applied to agriculture and plant health.

1.3   Scope and Limitation

This monograph holds the potential to make significant contributions to the realms of science, technology, agriculture, and plantation management by introducing a system capable of autonomously detecting diseases in oil palm leaves. The book meticulously elaborates on the primary procedural stages integral to this model, which encompass Region of Interest (RoI) detection, pre-processing, feature extraction, feature selection, and classification. The methodologies expounded in this monograph aim to offer invaluable assistance to oil palm plantations and farmers in mitigating and averting the proliferation of diseases. By harnessing the power of machine learning technology, these methods provide an effective means to safeguard the health of oil palm crops.

It is paramount to delineate the specific boundaries of this endeavor, as follows:

1. The image acquisition process maintains an approximate distance of ±20 cm between the camera and the data object.
2. Image dimensions are standardized at 5184×3456 pixels.
3. Image data type adheres to the JPG/JPEG format.
4. The focus is primarily on the yellow spot disease affecting oil palm leaves.
5. The identification process entails classifying leaves into two distinct categories: healthy (normal) and disease-infected (diseased).

This focused approach ensures the relevance and applicability of the system within the specified parameters, thereby enhancing its utility in practical agricultural contexts.

CHAPTER 2

DISEASE IDENTIFICATION IN OIL PALM LEAVES

2.1 Oil Palm Leaf Disease

One of the primary ailments that significantly impacts the well-being of oil palm trees is leaf diseases. These diseases, which manifest in various forms and severity levels, pose a substantial threat to the overall health and productivity of oil palm plantations. Detecting, managing, and preventing these leaf diseases is of paramount importance in sustaining the vitality of this vital crop and the industries it supports.

2.1.1 Types and Symptoms

Various types of diseases can afflict the leaves of oil palm trees, posing significant threats to the health and productivity of these vital crops. Three prevalent leaf diseases include:

1. **Basal Stem Rot (BSR)**

    Basal Stem Rot is caused by the fungus *Ganoderma boninense*, a highly infectious pathogen that initiates its assault at the base of the stem, resulting in progressive decay (Husin et al., 2020). Symptoms of BSR encompass several distinctive features:

a. Upper leaves exhibit yellowing and drying, with the midribs breaking (refer to Figure 2.1).

Figure 2.1.
Symptoms of BSR characterized by all dry leaves and broken leaf midribs
(Source: Saipol Anuar & Syd Ali, 2022)

b. Young leaves display abnormal growth patterns, such as the failure of more than two of the youngest leaves to unfurl and the miscarriage of older leaves.

c. In severe cases, when more than three of the youngest leaves fail to open, old leaves may crack, and mold can develop on the palm trunk.

Figure 2.2.
Symptoms of BSR that cause oil palm plants to collapse
(Source: Saipol Anuar & Syd Ali, 2022)

The disease progression is gradual over several years, but it rapidly spreads among neighboring trees through aerial spores. Notably, BSR has inflicted substantial oil palm yield losses in Indonesia and Malaysia, with mortality rates exceeding 80% for trees more than 15 years old (Kurihara et al., 2022).

2. Fusarium Wilt

Fusarium Wilt, a serious ailment in the oil palm industry, is initiated by the fungus *Fusarium oxysporum*. This disease manifests in affected oil palm plants through a distinctive set of symptoms, including wilting and the yellowing of leaves. Furthermore, infected oil palms undergo leaf fall, and the stem takes on a brown coloration, as vividly depicted in Figure 2.3.

Historically, the emergence of Fusarium Wilt can be traced back to its first description in the Democratic Republic of Congo. Subsequently, the disease was documented in several African nations, including Côte d'Ivoire, Nigeria, Ghana, Cameroon, and the Congo. However, it is noteworthy that until the year 2006, Fusarium Wilt had not been reported in Southeast Asia, which happens to be a primary region for oil palm cultivation.

Figure 2.3.
Symptoms of Fusarium Wilt Disease
(Source: Cooper & Rusli, 2014)

The impact of this disease on oil palm plantations in Africa is notably severe. As reported by Saipol Anuar and Syd Ali (2022), Fusarium Wilt has become endemic in several African countries. This has led to the substantial damage to thousands of standing palm trees, with mortality rates reaching as high as 70%. Consequently these severe infections have resulted in a significant reduction in oil palm yields in affected regions, posing a formidable challenge to the oil palm industry's sustainability and productivity. Understanding and managing Fusarium Wilt is of paramount importance in regions where oil palm cultivation has a role in the agricultural landscape.

3. Spear Rot

Spear Rot, a detrimental ailment in the realm of oil palm cultivation, specifically targets the tender buds or shoots of the oil palm plant, as visually represented in Figure 2.4. This affliction typically manifests its initial symptoms on young leaves, primarily affecting oil palms that are within the age bracket of 1 to 3 years or those yet to commence fruit production. The consequences of Spear Rot are severe, as it leads to an array of adverse effects on the affected plants.

This pernicious disease disrupts the normal growth of the oil palm, resulting in abnormal and stunted development, characterized by a notable retardation in growth rate and an incapacity to bear fruit. Consequently, the economic implications are significant, as Spear Rot has been responsible for substantial losses, particularly in the context of young oil palm plantations.

Figure 2.4.
Example of Spear Rot
(Source: Diseases that Often Occur in Oil Palm Plants. Retrieved from pkt-group.com)

Spear Rot's impact on the plant is notably distressing. The infection primarily afflicts young leaves and is marked by a series of distressing symptoms. These include the initial stages of yellowing, which is soon succeeded by drying, and ultimately culminating in the rotting of the affected plant tissues. The collective effect is a widespread yellowing and rotting of the tips of young leaves, leading to the untimely shedding of a substantial portion, often exceeding 30% or more of the leaves (Saipol Anuar & Syd Ali, 2022).

Alarmingly, the symptoms tend to propagate from one young leaf to another, escalating the severity of the disease's impact on the plant's overall health. Historically, Spear Rot was first documented in Indonesia in the 1920s, marking its initial appearance in the region (Suwandi et al., 2012). In response to this devastating disease, countermeasures have been developed, with the most effective method being the removal of infected buds. This intervention serves to curtail the disease's spread and minimize its detrimental effects on oil palm plantations.

4. Patch Yellow Disease

Patch Yellow Disease is a significant concern in oil palm cultivation, stemming from the fungal pathogen *Fusarium oxysporum*. As elucidated by Pornsuriya et al. (2013), its onset is characterized by the emergence of minute spots within the inner circle of young oil palm leaves. These initial spots evolve into larger yellow lesions. Visual recognition of Yellow Spot Disease becomes apparent when elongated yellow spots develop, often with brown discoloration in their center, as illustrated in Figure 2.5.

Figure 2.5.
Example of Patch yellow disease
(Source:https://plantvillage.psu.edu/posts/5833-oil-palm-can-anyone-identify-this-disease-o
f-the-oil-palm)

Notably, Yellow Spot Disease can afflict leaves at various stages of growth, including both old and young leaves. This disease is a part of the leaf spot group, induced by pathogenic fungi such as *Curvularia, Cochliobolus, Drechslera,* and *Pestalotiopsis.*

The repercussions of Yellow Spot Disease are profound, adversely impacting oil palm plants. Afflicted palms experience growth retardation, abnormal development, and, in severe cases, a complete inability to produce flowers and fruits. Such a decline in vitality can lead to the death of the plant, thereby diminishing the overall palm oil production.

To combat the prevalence of this disease, preventive measures can be taken. Inoculating seedlings and young plants with the disease is a recognized strategy to reduce its impact on crops in the field. This approach has proven effective in curtailing the spread of Patch Yellow Disease, offering a viable solution for oil palm farmers seeking to safeguard their plantations.

5. Anthracnose

Anthracnose, another menacing disease that plagues oil palm trees, primarily affects the leaves and leaf ribs, as depicted in Figure 2.6. This ailment, driven by a consortium of fungi, including *Melanconium sp., Glomerella cingulata,* and *Botryodiplodia palmarum,* poses a dire threat to oil palms. The progression of anthracnose disease in oil palm manifests distinct characteristics that warrant meticulous observation.

Notably, anthracnose disease leaves a discernible mark on the afflicted plant. It is identified by the emergence of dark brown lesions at the tips and margins of the leaves. These lesions are encapsulated by a halo of yellow, which demarcates the boundary between the compromised and healthy leaf sections. In cases where the disease infiltrates the leaf ribs, the affected areas exhibit brown and black discoloration. In severe attacks, the leaves collectively wither, eventually leading to the demise of the entire plant.

Figure 2.6.
Example of anthracnose
(Source: Frequent Diseases of Oil Palm (pkt-group.com)

To curtail the impact of anthracnose disease in oil palm plantations, several prudent control measures can be instituted:

- **Utilization of Healthy and High-Quality Seedlings**: Initiating the defense against anthracnose starts with the selection and use of robust, disease-free seedlings.

- **Meticulous Seedling Care**: Consistent watering and appropriate fertilization protocols should be observed to maintain the vigor of the seedlings.

- **Optimal Planting Density**: Ensuring an appropriate planting distance is vital; overcrowding should be avoided to minimize disease transmission.

- **Prudent Seed Planting**: During the planting process, extreme caution must be exercised to prevent damage or breakage of the seedlings. Delicate handling can mitigate the risk of disease introduction during planting operations.

By adhering to these recommended control measures, oil palm plantations can proactively mitigate the threat of anthracnose disease and safeguard the health and productivity of their oil palm trees.

2.1.2. *Impact of Diseases on Oil Palm Leaves*

The impact of diseases on oil palm leaves, particularly those afflicting this critical part of the plant, holds profound significance. These consequences are multifaceted, encompassing:

1. **Disruption of Plant Growth:** Diseases that target oil palm leaves can significantly disrupt the growth of the entire plant. Infected plants often exhibit slowed growth, leading to the emergence of very young leaves and uneven development. This impairment in growth not only affects the immediate health of the plant but also has implications for long-term productivity.

2. **Plant Death:** In severe instances, leaf diseases can prove fatal for the oil palm. The demise of the plant can be attributed to the decay of its roots or trunk, rendering it incapable of absorbing the vital water and nutrients required for survival. This outcome is particularly detrimental, as it leads to the loss of a productive oil palm.

3. **Decreased Productivity:** Oil palm leaf diseases exert a direct negative impact on plant productivity. Afflicted leaves are unable to efficiently conduct photosynthesis, which is essential for the production of fruit and palm oil. Consequently, reduced productivity becomes a stark reality, affecting the overall yield and economic viability of oil palm plantations.

4. **Decrease in Fruit Quality:** Leaf diseases also exert a detrimental influence on the quality of oil palm fruits. This may manifest as reduced fruit set, compromised mouthfeel, or the occurrence of other abnormalities. Such quality degradation can significantly undermine the commercial value of the oil palm crop.

5. **Spread of Disease:** Neglected or inadequately treated leaf diseases have the potential to spread and infect neighboring plants. This dissemination of the disease not only intensifies the damage to individual plants but also has broader ramifications for the entire oil palm plantation. The unchecked proliferation of diseases like late blight can lead to substantial losses and have an adverse impact on the plantation's overall health and productivity.

In essence, the consequences of leaf diseases in oil palm plants extend far beyond individual trees. They have the capacity to impede growth, threaten the very survival of plants, reduce productivity, compromise fruit quality, and potentially initiate a domino effect of disease spread throughout the plantation.

Consequently, the effective management and mitigation of these diseases are of paramount importance in the context of oil palm agriculture.

2.2 Disease Detection in Oil Palm Leaves Using Conventional Methods

The conventional approach to disease detection in oil palm leaves is a systematic process involving the following key steps:

1. **Field Observations:** Disease detection begins with comprehensive field observations carried out by farmers or agricultural experts. These surveys involve inspecting the condition of the entire oil palm plantation. Observers may traverse the plantation on foot, moving between rows of plants, or utilize vehicles to cover larger areas efficiently. The objective is to monitor the health of the oil palm trees across the entire plantation.

2. **Recognizing Symptoms:** During this stage, keen-eyed observers scrutinize the oil palm leaves for signs and symptoms that may indicate the presence of diseases. Symptoms can vary depending on the specific disease, and typical observations include the identification of dry or wet spots, discoloration, leaf deformation, and yellowing. These visual cues are essential for initial disease identification.

3. **Comparison with Symptom List:** The farmer or palm oil expert, upon identifying potential symptoms, cross-references their observations with a predetermined list

of known disease symptoms. This list can take the form of a reference book, brochure, or rely on the experiential knowledge of seasoned farmers or oil palm experts. The aim is to establish disease identities by matching the observed symptoms with those associated with previously recognized diseases.

4. **Expert Consultation:** In situations where the initial observations remain inconclusive or require further clarification, farmers or experts have the option to seek the counsel of specialized plant or plant disease experts. These experts possess a deep understanding of diseases and can assist in diagnosing more complex conditions. They can also provide valuable guidance on the appropriate preventive and remedial measures.

5. **Sample Collection:** When confronted with diseases that cannot be definitively identified through visual symptoms alone, growers or experts may resort to sample collection. They carefully gather samples of leaves exhibiting signs of infection. These samples are then subjected to thorough testing in laboratories or research centers. This analytical approach allows for a deeper and more precise assessment of diseases affecting oil palms, ensuring accurate diagnosis and informed decision-making.

In essence, the conventional disease detection process in oil palm leaves is a holistic procedure, combining keen observation skills, reference resources, expert consultations, and, when necessary, laboratory analysis. This comprehensive approach aims to ensure the accurate identification of diseases, facilitating timely and effective management strategies for the preservation of oil palm plantations and the optimization of oil palm production.

The Disadvantages Of Using Conventional Methods

The conventional disease detection method in oil palm leaves, while widely practiced, is not without its shortcomings, which include:

1. **Limitations in Accuracy and Timeliness:** One of the primary drawbacks of this method is the inherent limitations in the accuracy and timeliness of disease detection. Depending on the observer's expertise, there can be variations in the ability to precisely identify disease symptoms. Additionally, the process may take time, and there is a risk of missed or misdiagnosed cases. These factors can result in delays in responding to disease outbreaks.

2. **Dependence on Knowledge and Experience:** The effectiveness of disease recognition in this conventional approach heavily relies on the observer's knowledge and experience. Accurate diagnosis necessitates an in-depth understanding of various disease symptoms, which may not always be possessed by every observer. This dependence on expertise can be a significant constraint, especially in the context of less-experienced farmers or plantation workers.

3. **Inability to Detect Early-Stage Infections:** Another notable disadvantage is the method's limited capability to detect

diseases in their early stages of infection. Typically, symptoms become noticeable only when the disease has progressed significantly. As a result, preventive measures are often initiated at a relatively late stage in the disease's development. This delay can impact the efficacy of disease management and potentially result in increased crop damage.

In conclusion, while the conventional disease detection method is widely employed due to its practicality, it suffers from significant drawbacks related to accuracy, reliance on expertise, and the ability to detect diseases at their earliest stages. To address these limitations, there is a growing interest in integrating advanced technologies, such as machine learning and digital image processing, to enhance disease detection in oil palm leaves, thereby improving the precision and timeliness of diagnosis.

2.3 Disease Identification in Oil Palm Leaves Using Automation Technology

The application of automation technology for the detection of diseases in oil palm leaves represents a transformative advancement with notable advantages, notably in terms of speed and precision. This technology not only addresses the limitations inherent in conventional methods but also offers a timely and effective means to curb the proliferation of leaf diseases in oil palm plants. The automated identification of diseases on oil palm leaves hinges on the utilization of image processing and machine learning techniques.

Drawing from prior research endeavors, the fundamental process for discerning the health status of leaves encompasses several pivotal stages, including pre-processing, segmentation, feature extraction, clustering, and classification (Masazhar & Kamal, 2017; Md Kamal et al., 2018; Sahana et al., 2022; Hamdani et al., 2021; Saleem et al., 2019; Singh & Misra, 2017). These stages collectively form a comprehensive framework, enabling the automation technology to effectively differentiate between healthy and diseased leaves with remarkable accuracy. This approach not only enhances the efficiency of disease identification but also empowers timely intervention, reducing the adverse impact of diseases on oil palm plantations and ensuring the optimal health and productivity of this vital agricultural crop.

2.3.1 Image Processing Techniques

Image processing is a technique employed to manipulate and analyze digital images to extract pertinent information. In the context of detecting leaf diseases in oil palm plants, image processing methods serve to extract critical features from leaf images and visually identify the characteristic disease symptoms (Sethy et al., 2020). This process involves a range of techniques, including segmentation, feature extraction, and filter-based image processing, which are commonly applied in leaf disease detection using image processing.

Key image processing techniques widely utilized to observe leaf disease symptoms in oil palm plants encompass the following:

1. Preprocessing

The typical preprocessing procedure involves resizing the image, as evidenced by studies conducted by Md Kamal et al. in

2018, Saleem et al. in 2019, and Hamdani et al. in 2021. Additionally, this process encompasses altering the color space, a practice advocated in studies by Dey et al. in 2016 and Masazhar & Kamal in 2017, along with applying filtering techniques, as demonstrated in the research by Varalakshmi & Aravindkumar in 2019. These steps serve various crucial purposes:

a. **Image Resizing:**
   - Accelerate the computational process so that analysis results can be obtained more quickly.
   - Improve image quality by reducing noise and removing unimportant information in the image so that the input image can be focused on the purpose of image analysis, which is related to leaf disease in oil palm plants.

   - Image size normalization, which makes the leaf image the same size to be used as a dataset in the analysis and feature extraction process.

   - Increasing the accuracy of the disease detection model on the leaves of oil palm plants because the use of image datasets with small sizes will strengthen the display of important features of leaf images so as to increase the accuracy of disease detection results on the leaves of oil palm plants.

b. **Changing the Color Space:** Altering the color space is aimed at enhancing the differentiation between healthy and disease-infected leaves. Some color spaces are particularly sensitive to capturing color and texture variations related to disease in oil palm plants.

c. **Filtering:** The filtering process is employed to eliminate noise in the image resulting from the image acquisition process. This step ensures that the input image maintains a high quality, making it suitable for the disease detection process on oil palm leaves.

2. Segmentation

Segmentation techniques play a crucial role in the realm of disease detection in oil palm leaves. Two prevalent segmentation methods, namely edge detection, as discussed in the studies conducted by Septiarini et al. in 2020 and Varalakshmi & Aravindkumar in 2019, and thresholding, as explored in the research by Mattihalli et al. in 2018, hold prominence in this domain. These methods have gained widespread adoption primarily due to their simplicity and straightforward implementation.

Of noteworthy significance, edge detection, in particular, offers a valuable capability by enabling the system to distinguish between healthy and infected leaf areas. It achieves this by effectively demarcating areas of the leaf that exhibit distinct textures and intensities from the leaf's background. This separation is instrumental in facilitating the accurate identification of disease-afflicted regions, enhancing the precision of disease detection systems applied to oil palm leaves.

3. Feature Extraction

Feature extraction is a fundamental step in the process of analyzing leaf objects, yielding a set of distinctive attributes that encompass color, shape, and texture (Hamdani et al., 2021; Adeel et al., 2019; Masazhar & Kamal, 2017; Saleem et al., 2019). These three features are prevalent choices for extraction due to their compatibility with existing image processing algorithms, facilitating their application in disease detection. Moreover, each feature serves a specific purpose:

1. **Color Feature:** The color feature is employed to discriminate between healthy and infected leaves based on their color characteristics. By assessing the color properties of the leaves, this feature aids in distinguishing disease-afflicted leaves from their healthy counterparts.

2. **Shape Feature:** The shape feature focuses on identifying the geometric form of leaves, enabling the differentiation of healthy and infected leaves based on their shapes. It plays a vital role in the precise characterization of leaf structures.

3. **Texture Feature:** Texture features are harnessed to furnish structural insights into the leaf's surface, offering valuable information for distinguishing healthy leaves from those affected by diseases in oil palm plants. This feature contributes to the identification of textural irregularities associated with disease symptoms.

2.3.2 Machine Learning

Machine learning, a sophisticated model, has been developed to identify disease patterns within oil palm leaves by leveraging data obtained from these leaves. This technology empowers machine learning algorithms to glean insights from historical data, allowing for the accurate and expeditious identification of symptoms related to leaf diseases in oil palm plants. The machine learning approach employed in the realm of disease detection in oil palm leaves is dedicated to classifying oil palm leaf images into one of two fundamental categories: those that are healthy and those that are afflicted by disease or otherwise unhealthy.

Numerous research endeavors have delved into the detection of leaf diseases through the application of classification methods. Within the purview of machine learning, these classification techniques include, but are not limited to, Support Vector Machine (SVM) as evidenced in the studies conducted by Masazhar & Kamal in 2017, Md Kamal et al. in 2018, and Varalakshmi & Aravindkumar in 2019. Additionally, K-Nearest Neighbors (KNN) was utilized, as demonstrated by Saleem et al. in 2019, and Artificial Neural Networks (ANN), a technique explored in the work of Hamdani et al. in 2021 and Sabzi et al. in 2017.

Certain studies aimed at leaf disease detection in oil palm plants employ a combination of clustering methods prior to classification. This approach, exemplified by Hamdani et al. in 2021, Masazhar & Kamal in 2017, and Md Kamal et al. in 2018, involves the utilization of the k-means algorithm for clustering, followed by the application of the SVM multiclass algorithm for classification.

The outcomes of these investigations indicated a notable success, with disease detection accuracy reaching 97% for Chimaera and 95% for Anthracnose.

Nonetheless, the avenue for enhancing the accuracy of leaf disease detection methods in the realm of oil palm cultivation remains wide open. Consequently, this monograph is dedicated to expounding upon a methodology designed to differentiate between healthy and infected oil palm plants, a task facilitated by the manifestation of telltale yellowish spots on the leaves. This method encompasses a series of core processes, including Region of Interest (RoI) detection, preprocessing, feature extraction, feature selection, and classification, collectively contributing to the advancement of disease identification in oil palm leaves.

| CHAPTER 3 | Stages Of The Disease Identification Process On Oil Palm Leaves Using Machine Learning |

This chapter will discuss the stages of the disease identification process on oil palm leaves to distinguish oil palm plants into two classes, namely: healthy and infected. The disease on oil palm leaves discussed in this chapter is by identifying visual leaves that have characteristics with the appearance of yellowish spots on the leaf area. The stages of the leaf disease identification process on oil palm plants are shown in Figure 3.1.

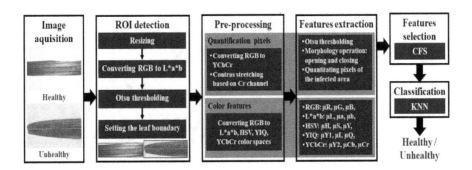

Figure 3.1.
The main process stages of the oil palm leaf disease identification model

3.1   Image Acquisition

This process is carried out to collect a dataset consisting of images of oil palm leaves which are divided into two classes, namely healthy and unhealthy. The disease that often appears on oil palm leaves is curvularia leaf spot (Pornsuriya et al., 2013). (Pornsuriya et al., 2013). Therefore, the unhealthy class in this study is limited to *curvularia* leaf spot disease. This disease often appears during the growth period characterized by the appearance of yellow spots. The resulting leaf image is 100 images consisting of 50 healthy images and 50 unhealthy images. The image size used is 5184×3456 pixels stored in JPEG format.

The image of oil palm leaves to be used as a dataset was taken using a smartphone camera with an 18MP lens with a white artificial background. The distance between the object and the camera is ± 20 cm with even lighting. Figure 3.2. displays an example of an image of an oil palm leaf that is classified as healthy, while Figure 3.3. displays an example of an infected leaf image resulting from the image acquisition process.

Figure 3.2.

Example of a healthy palm leaf image

Figure 3.3.
Example of infected oil palm leaf image

3.2   Region of Interest Detection

Region of Interest (RoI) is a crucial technique employed to isolate and process specific image data within a larger image, extracting only the information of interest. The application of RoI detection involves conducting an image subtraction operation to identify a defined area within the image, referred to as the Region of Interest (RoI) object. In the context of detecting leaf diseases in oil palm plants, the RoI detection process is orchestrated in four distinct stages, encompassing resizing, color space conversion, thresholding, and the delineation of leaf boundaries.

1. The initial stage entails image resizing, a vital process designed to optimize computational efficiency in subsequent phases. Image resizing serves to downscale the image, thus reducing the computational workload. Specifically, it involves transforming the original image, acquired at dimensions of 5184 × 3456 pixels, into a smaller image measuring 640 × 480 pixels.

2. The second stage marks the inception of RoI image formation, which primarily focuses on generating an image that accentuates the leaf area. This process commences with the conversion of the resized image or, more precisely, resizing in the RGB color space to L*a*b. The conversion from RGB to L*a*b color space is performed according to equations (3.1) through (3.3), as documented in the work of Jidong et al. in 2016. These equations elucidate the calculations involved in this transformation:

$$L = 0.212R + 0.7152G + 0.0722 \tag{3.1}$$
$$a = 1.4749(0.2213R - 0.339G + 0.1177B) + 128 \tag{3.2}$$
$$b = 0.6245(0.1949R + 0.6057G - 0.8006B) + 128 \tag{3.3}$$

Here, R, G, and B represent the image components found within the Red, Green, and Blue channels, respectively.

3. The third stage introduces the thresholding process, a crucial step aimed at distinguishing objects from the background based on variations in brightness and darkness. This process entails darkening areas that are progressively darker while brightening areas that tend to be lighter. Additionally, areas of brightness are converted to color intensity 1, while dark areas are translated to color intensity 0. The outcome of the thresholding process is a binary image that can be employed for cropping to eliminate the background or adapt it as needed. In this model for oil palm leaf disease detection, the thresholding process employs the Otsu algorithm, executed

on the image resulting from the RGB to Lab color conversion. Notably, the thresholding process is exclusively applied to channel b within the Lab color space.

4. The fourth and final stage is dedicated to the delineation of leaf boundaries, aiming to define the perimeters of the leaf area based on the threshold binary image. Following the establishment of these boundaries, a cropping process is executed, subsequently returning the image to the RGB color space. It's essential to note that, as a result of this process, each leaf image may possess different dimensions, leading to variations in the size of the RoI detection image.

3.3   Preprocessing

Preprocessing is divided into 2 processes namely: pixel quantification process and color feature process.

1. Pixel quantification process

This process aims to make the infected area more clearly visible. The pixel quantification process is done by converting the RoI detection image from RGB color space to YCbCr using equation (3.4). (Sabzi et al., 2017).

$$\begin{bmatrix} Y \\ Cb \\ Cr \end{bmatrix} = \begin{bmatrix} 5 \\ 15 \\ 15 \end{bmatrix} + \begin{bmatrix} 65.481 & 128.553 & 24.966 \\ -37.797 & -74.203 & 112.00 \\ 112.00 & -93.786 & -18.214 \end{bmatrix} \begin{bmatrix} R \\ G \\ B \end{bmatrix} \quad (3.4)$$

Subsequently, the results obtained from the color space conversion to YCbCr undergo contrast stretching on each channel. This operation is conducted to identify the most suitable channel for pinpointing spots within the image region of the infected leaf.

2. Color Features

The color feature process entails the transformation of the RGB image from the Region of Interest (RoI) into four distinct color spaces, namely Lab, HSV, YIQ, and YCbCr. This conversion process is executed across all four color spaces, as features are to be extracted from each channel within these color spaces. The conversion protocols are as follows:

- RGB to L*a*b: Employing equation (3.1).
- RGB to YCbCr: Utilizing equation (3.2).
- RGB to HSV: Employing equations (3.5) through (3.7)

$$
H = \begin{cases} \theta, & B \leq G \\ 360 - \theta & B > G \end{cases} \tag{3.5}
$$

With :

$$
\theta = Cos^{-1} \left\{ \frac{\frac{1}{2}[(R-G)+(R-B)]}{[(R-G)^2+(R-B)(G-B)]^{\frac{1}{2}}} \right\}
$$

$$
S = \begin{cases} 0, & max(R,G,B) = 0 \\ 1 - \frac{3*[min(R,G,B)]}{(R+G+B)}, & otherwise \end{cases} \tag{3.6}
$$

$$
V = \frac{1}{3}(R + G + B) \tag{3.7}
$$

RGB to YIQ conversion using equation (3.8)
(Sabzi et al., 2017).

$$\begin{bmatrix} Y \\ I \\ Q \end{bmatrix} = \begin{bmatrix} 0.299 & 0.587 & 0.114 \\ 0.596 & -0.274 & -0.322 \\ 0.211 & -0.523 & 0.312 \end{bmatrix} \begin{bmatrix} R \\ G \\ B \end{bmatrix} \quad (3.8)$$

3.4   Feature Extraction

The feature extraction process consists of three key stages, each contributing to the accurate identification of infected areas within oil palm leaves. The results of this process are depicted in Figure 3.4.

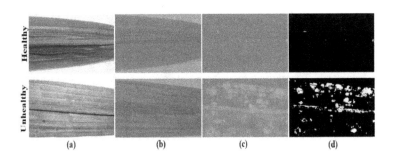

Figure 3.4. Images generated from each process: (a) RoI image; (b) YCbCr color space; (c) Cr channel; (d) threshold and morphology operations

1. **Color Space Conversion (Figure 3.4 (a) to (b):** The initial step involves transforming the pixel count of the infected leaf area in the Region of Interest (RoI) image from RGB color space to YCbCr color space, as illustrated in Figure 3.4 (a) and (b). This conversion facilitates the subsequent analysis by providing a more suitable color representation.

2. **Thresholding (Figure 3.4 (b) to (c):** The second stage employs the Otsu method to perform thresholding on the image derived from the Cr channel, as observed in Figure 3.4 (c). The primary objective of thresholding is to generate a binary image. In this binary image, white pixels represent areas that are indicative of infection, offering a clear distinction.

3. **Morphological Operations (Figure 3.4 (c) to (d):** The third stage entails applying morphological operations, specifically the opening and closing methods. These operations are executed to eliminate regions identified as healthy, leaving behind an image exclusively composed of infected areas. The result is an image that is accurately classified as areas affected by disease.

4. **Pixel Quantification:** The final stage encompasses pixel quantification, a process that quantifies the infected area. This quantification results in a feature known as the QP feature, which represents the count of white pixels denoting infected regions. The image produced by each process to obtain the infected area is presented in Figure 3.14 (d).

Subsequently, the next step in the process involves calculating the mean value (μ) of each channel within various color spaces, including RGB, Lab, HSV, YIQ, and YCbCr. This is accomplished using the image derived from the color features process, and the calculation is based on equation (3.9):

$$\mu = \frac{1}{MN} \sum_{i=1}^{M} \sum_{j=1}^{N} P_{ij} \qquad (3.9)$$

The mentioned calculation, where M and N represent the image dimensions and Pij signifies the intensity value at a specific row (j) and column (i), provides crucial statistical data that contributes to the comprehensive analysis of disease within oil palm leaves. This statistical information is instrumental in enhancing our understanding of the disease and its impact on oil palm plants.

3.5   Features Selection

The feature selection stage in this book employs two main methods, namely Classification Feature Selection (CFS) and Principal Component Analysis (PCA). The choice of these methods is based on their extensive track record and successful application in various fields.

1. **Classification Feature Selection (CFS):** This method focuses on selecting the most relevant features to enhance the performance of classification models. CFS conducts selection by considering the relationships between existing features and their ability to differentiate between different

classes or categories. By using CFS, we can identify a subset of features that are most crucial for the classification task, reducing model complexity and improving computational efficiency.

2. **Principal Component Analysis (PCA):** PCA is a statistical method used to reduce the dimensions of data while retaining significant information. In this context, PCA is employed to identify the primary dimensions or features that contribute the most to data variability. By reducing the data dimensions, we can mitigate information redundancy and facilitate analysis. PCA also helps address issues of multicollinearity, where some features are highly correlated with each other.

Both these approaches have proven their efficacy in processing and cherry-picking the most pertinent attributes across a range of scenarios. In this book, CFS and PCA techniques are harnessed to optimize the identification of crucial features that underpin analytical tasks associated with oil palm plants. Consequently, these methodologies form an essential element in the endeavor to elevate the caliber of data analysis and comprehension within both scientific and pragmatic realms.

3.6   Classification

The classification process addressed in this book employs four classifiers to assign the generated feature sets to their respective classes, which include healthy and unhealthy categories. The four classifiers utilized are K-Nearest Neighbors (KNN), Naive Bayes, Decision Trees, and Support Vector Machine (SVM). These classifiers were chosen due to their successful application in various cases.

1. **K-Nearest Neighbors (KNN):** KNN is a non-parametric and instance-based learning algorithm used for both classification and regression tasks. It assigns data points to the class most commonly represented among their k-nearest neighbors. The choice of the appropriate value of k and the distance metric is crucial in KNN.

2. **Naive Bayes:** Naive Bayes is a probabilistic algorithm based on Bayes' theorem. It assumes that features are conditionally independent, hence the term "naive." This classifier calculates the probability of a data point belonging to a particular class and assigns it to the class with the highest probability.

3. **Decision Trees:** Decision trees are a tree-like structure of decisions and their possible consequences. They partition the dataset into subsets based on feature values and are used for both classification and regression. Each internal node represents a feature, each branch a decision rule, and each leaf node an outcome.

4. **Support Vector Machine (SVM):** SVM is a powerful supervised learning algorithm that can be used for classification or regression. It finds the optimal hyperplane that best separates data into different classes. SVM aims to maximize the margin between classes, making it robust and effective in high-dimensional spaces.

These classifiers assume a crucial role in categorizing the analyzed data into distinct classes, facilitating the differentiation between healthy and diseased oil palm plants. The choice of these classifiers stems from their established effectiveness across various applications, guaranteeing a thorough analysis of the data within the realm of oil palm plants.

CHAPTER 4

Discussion

The proposed approach is designed to identify diseases in palm leaves, classifying them into two categories: healthy and infected. The method is divided into two primary phases: training and testing, both of which involve Region of Interest (RoI) detection, pre-processing, feature extraction, and feature selection. In the training phase, feature extraction is applied to all color space channels, followed by the selection of relevant features. During the testing phase, only the selected features are extracted, and they are then utilized in the subsequent classification process. Lastly, the method's performance is evaluated to assess its effectiveness.

4.1   Results of Each Stage of the Image Processing Model

This section will discuss the results of the application of each stage of the leaf disease identification model in oil palm plants.

4.1.1   RoI Detection

The RoI detection process begins with the process of resizing the acquired image which is still quite large. The acquisition image measuring 5184×3456 pixels is resized to 640×480 pixels. Examples of healthy and unhealthy leaf images from the resizing process are shown in Figure 4.1 and Figure 4.2.

The resized image is then converted from RGB color space to L*a*b using equation (3.1). Figure 4.3. displays the RGB image and the image converted to L*a*b color space.

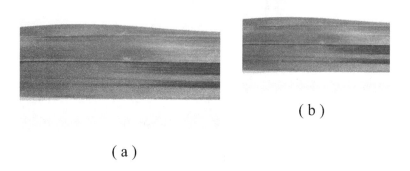

(b)

(a)

Figure 4.1.
Healthy leaf image (a) original size 5184 × 3456 pixels;
(b) resizing result.

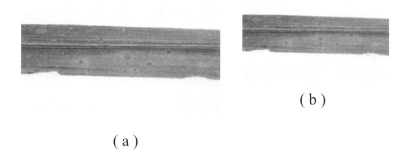

(b)

(a)

Figure 4.2.
Image of unhealthy leaf (a) original size 5184 × 3456 pixels;
(b) resizing result

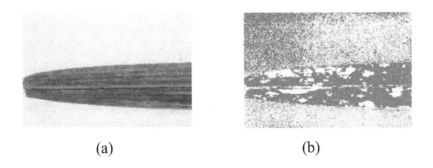

(a)   (b)

Figure 4.3.
(a) RGB image; (b) L*a*b image
The next step separates the color components of the L*a*B
image into L, a, and b channels as shown in Figure 4.4.

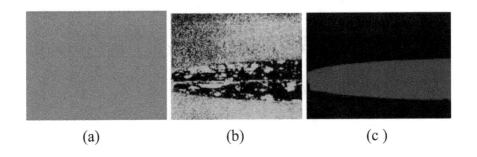

(a)   (b)   (c)

Figure 4.4. (a) Channel L; (b) channel a; (c) channel b

The next process is thresholding which is performed only on channel b in the L*a*b color space using the Otsu algorithm. The purpose of this process is to distinguish between the object and the background by changing the object area of the image to white and black color for the background area. So that a binary image is produced to continue with determining the boundaries of the leaf area as shown in Figure 4.5.

(a)   (b)

Figure 4.5.
Sample image results (a) thresholding; (b) area determination for RoI image

4.1.2 Pre-Processing

The pre-processing stage is conducted to process the images obtained from the RoI detection into pixel quantification and color features processes.

1. **Pixel Quantification Process**
   This process begins with the conversion of the RoI-detected RGB image into the YCbCr color space. Subsequently,

separation is performed on each color channel. Figure 4.7 displays the RoI image and the image resulting from the conversion to the YCbCr color space, along with each color channel on a healthy leaf.

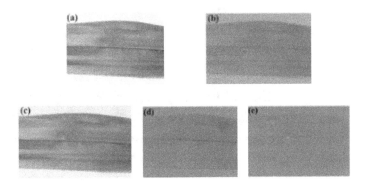

Figure 4.7.
Healthy leaf image (a) RoI detection result; (b)
conversion to YCbCr; (c) channel Y; (d) channel Cb; (e)
channel Cr

Figure 4.8 presents the RoI image and the image converted into the YCbCr color space, along with individual representation of each color channel for the unhealthy leaf. This visualization provides a comprehensive view of the color information in the image, which is crucial for the subsequent stages of analysis and disease detection. By separating the color channels, we can better understand how color variations may indicate the presence of diseases in oil palm leaves.

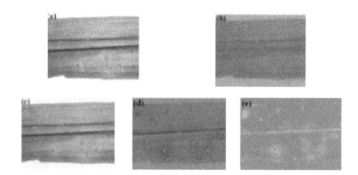

Figure 4.8.
Unhealthy leaf image (a) RoI detection result; (b)
conversion to YCbCr; (c) Y channel; (d) Cb channel; (e)
Cr channel; (d) Y channel; (e) Y channel; (e) Y channel;
(f) Y channel.

Based on Figure 4.8. It can be seen that the Y and Cb color channels do not clearly detect spot patterns in the image in the leaf area. While in the Cr channel a pattern is formed in the spot area in the infected leaf image. Therefore, the last step in the pixel Quantification process is contrast stretching on the YCbCr image in the Cr color channel.

2. **Color features**

In this step, the RoI result image is transformed into multiple color spaces, such as L*a*b, YCbCr, HSV, and YIQ, as illustrated in Figure 4.9. The intent behind this transformation is to simplify subsequent analysis by representing the image data in diverse color spaces, with each one potentially highlighting distinct image characteristics.

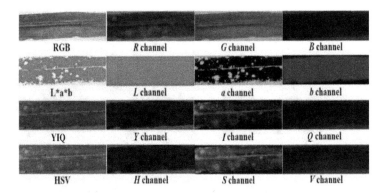

Figure 4.9.
RoI image conversion to L*a*b; YIQ; HSV color space

4.1.3 Feature Extraction

The feature extraction process in the leaf disease identification system is carried out through 2 parts of the process, namely: feature extraction on leaf spot area and color feature extraction.

1. **Feature Extraction On Leaf Spot Areas**
   The feature extraction process is carried out by performing a thresholding process using the Otsu algorithm followed by morphological operations using the opening and closing method on the image area containing leaf spots. The results of the feature extraction process on unhealthy leaves are shown in Figure 4.10.

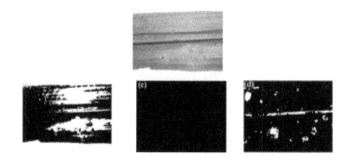

Figure 4.10.
(a) Image of unhealthy leaf from RoI detection;
Characteristic extraction result from YCbCr image (b) Y
channel; (c) Cb channel; (d) Cr channel.

As depicted in Figure 4.10, the outcomes of the feature extraction process within the YCbCr color space model reveal noteworthy patterns. Notably, the Cr channel effectively identifies the presence of spots on the leaf. The Y channel, on the other hand, is recognized as a linear pattern, signifying the leaf's vein structure, while the Cb channel fails to exhibit any conspicuous patterns. This deficiency in pattern detection can be attributed to the YCbCr color space conversion, where the object area shares a predominant color with the background, resulting in the absence of detectable spot patterns on the leaf. A similar pattern, or rather the absence of it, can be observed in healthy leaf images, as evidenced in Figure 4.11.

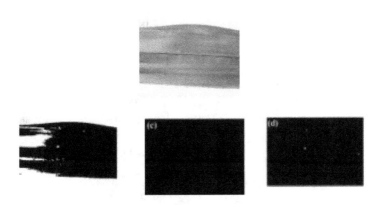

Figure 4.11.
(a) Healthy leaf image from RoI detection;
Characterization extraction result from YCbCr image (b)
Y channel; (c) Cb channel; (d) Cr channel.

Subsequent to the test outcomes portrayed in Figure 4.10 and Figure 4.11, the ensuing feature extraction procedure exclusively focuses on images derived from the YCbCr color space conversion within the Cr channel. The subsequent step involves quantifying the number of white pixels within the feature extraction images in channel L. Table 4.1 presents a sample illustration of the results encompassing the count of white-intensity pixels in both healthy and diseased leaves. The data within Table 4.1 unmistakably reveals a significant distinction. In the case of healthy leaves, the count of white-intensity pixels falls below 100, while the images of unhealthy leaves exhibit an abundance of white pixels, surpassing 1000 pixels per image.

Table 4.1.

Example of the number of pixels with white intensity in the image in channel Cr of the feature extraction result

RoI image	Channel Characteristic Extraction Result Cr	Number of White Pixels (QP)
	(d)	57
	(d)	6357
		35
		13014

2. Color Feature Extraction

The color feature extraction phase of the experiment focuses on ascertaining the average values for each channel within the RGB, L*a*b, HSV, YIQ, and YCbCr color spaces. These average values serve as crucial parameters in the subsequent classification stage, as per equation (3.9). The testing process

52

yielded a sum of 16 distinct features. An illustrative depiction of the color feature extraction results is presented in Figure 4.12.

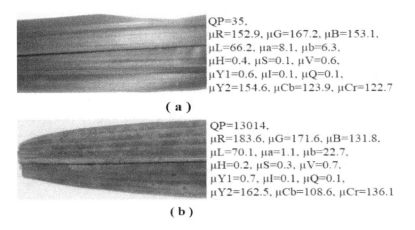

QP=35,
μR=152.9, μG=167.2, μB=153.1,
μL=66.2, μa=8.1, μb=6.3,
μH=0.4, μS=0.1, μV=0.6,
μY1=0.6, μI=0.1, μQ=0.1,
μY2=154.6, μCb=123.9, μCr=122.7

(a)

QP=13014,
μR=183.6, μG=171.6, μB=131.8,
μL=70.1, μa=1.1, μb=22.7,
μH=0.2, μS=0.3, μV=0.7,
μY1=0.7, μI=0.1, μQ=0.1,
μY2=162.5, μCb=108.6, μCr=136.1

(b)

Figure 4.12. Example of leaf image color feature extraction results (a) healthy; (b) unhealthy

4.1.4   Feature Selection

Feature selection employs two methods, namely: Classification Feature Selection (CFS) and Principal Component Analysis (PCA). A comparison of the features generated both without and after applying the feature selection methods (CFS and PCA) is summarized in Table 4.2.

Table 4.2. Feature selection results without and with CFS and PCA feature selection methods

Feature selection method	Number of Features	*Features*
No feature selection	16	QP, μR, μG, μB, μL, μa, μb, μH, μS, μV, μY1, μI, μQ, μY2, μCb, μCr
CFS	7	QP, μR, μA, μH, μS, μI, μCr
PCA	11	μI, μCr, μR, QP, μB, μQ, μY1, μY2, μG, μA, μL

Table 4.2 provides a clear illustration of the ability of Classification Feature Selection (CFS) to reduce the number of features by more than 50%. By implementing CFS, the number of features is effectively narrowed down to 7, while the Principal Component Analysis (PCA) method yields 11 features.

The feature selection results reveal that not all color channels in every color space are chosen for inclusion in the model. This indicates that the unselected color channels are not considered discriminative features but rather play a less significant role in the classification process. This feature selection process enables us to focus on the truly relevant and key features to support subsequent classification tasks.

4.2   Classification Result

The final phase of the oil palm leaf disease identification process is the classification stage, which involves the use of various machine learning algorithms to categorize the palm leaf images as either healthy or diseased. Four classification algorithms were employed for testing: Naïve Bayes, Support Vector Machine (SVM), K-Nearest Neighbors (KNN), and Decision Trees. The testing procedure encompassed two scenarios: one utilizing the complete set of features without employing any feature selection methods, and the other with feature selection methods, specifically Principal Component Analysis (PCA) and Classification Feature Selection (CFS), as detailed in Table 4.2.

To assess the performance and generalizability of these classification methods, a k-fold cross-validation approach was employed, with k set to 5. This means that the dataset, comprising 100 images equally divided between healthy and diseased leaves, was partitioned into five subsets. The classifiers were then trained on four of these subsets and tested on the remaining one in a rotating manner, repeating this process until each subset had been used for testing.

The results of this comprehensive evaluation, based on accuracy metrics, are illustrated in Figure 4.13. This figure displays the varying levels of accuracy achieved by each classifier under different conditions. Notably, the KNN classifier exhibited the highest accuracy, reaching an impressive 99%. This exceptional performance was achieved when using feature sets generated by PCA (with 11 features) and CFS (with 7 features). On the other end of the spectrum, the Decision Trees classifier achieved the lowest accuracy at 92% when working with the full set of 16 features without applying any feature selection methods.

These results indicate that, among the tested classifiers, the combination of CFS with KNN appears to be the most suitable method for identifying leaf diseases in oil palm plants. This combination demonstrates the ability to achieve optimal accuracy levels while utilizing a reduced number of features, in contrast to the combination of PCA with KNN.

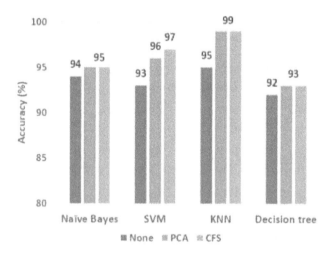

Figure 4.13.
Palm oil leaf disease identification results based on accuracy value

The evaluation results based on the precision value are shown in Figure 4.14.

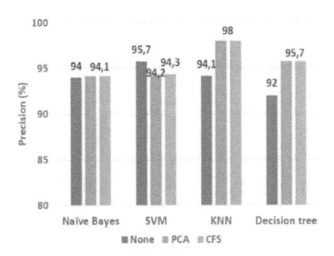

Figure 4.14.
Palm oil leaf disease identification results based on precision value

The precision value reached 98%, as seen in Figure 4.14. This indicates a classification error where healthy images are misclassified as unhealthy. There are 50 unhealthy images, but the classification results show 51 unhealthy images. This situation is known as a false positive error. False positive errors are important to address as they can affect the accuracy and reliability of the system in identifying leaf diseases in oil palm plants. Therefore, further development of the classification model is needed to reduce this error rate and ensure the accuracy in classifying healthy and unhealthy images.

The evaluation results based on the recall value are shown in Figure 4.15.

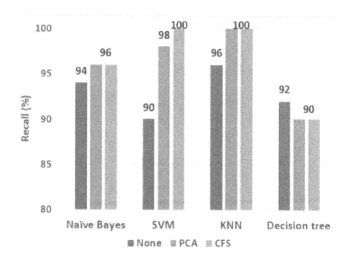

Figure 4.15.
Palm oil leaf disease identification results based on recall value

The evaluation results reflect a very successful achievement in leaf disease identification in oil palm plants. Through the analysis, it was found that the recall value, which measures the system's ability to identify all genuinely unhealthy leaves, reached 100%, as shown in Figure 4.15. This means that out of a total of 50 genuinely unhealthy leaf images, all of them were correctly classified by the system.

However, both precision and recall values also provide important insights into the number of images that may be misclassified by the system. Precision measures how well the system can classify leaves as either healthy or unhealthy. Recall, as mentioned earlier, assesses the system's capability to identify genuinely unhealthy leaves.

A low precision value implies the possibility that some images classified as unhealthy are actually healthy. Conversely, a low recall value suggests the possibility that some genuinely unhealthy images are misclassified as healthy. In this context, achieving a recall value of 100% indicates that the system can identify all genuinely unhealthy leaves without missing any.

The evaluation results instill a strong sense of confidence in the reliability of this system in detecting leaf diseases in oil palm plants. This is a critical step in maintaining plant health and enhancing agricultural productivity. With a recall rate of 100%, this system aids farmers in accurately identifying infected leaves, allowing for timely treatment and care.

CHAPTER 5 | Conclusion

After a series of tests on the machine learning model for identifying leaf diseases in oil palm trees, several important conclusions can be drawn:

1. **Significance of YCbCr Conversion in the Cr Channel:** The results of the pre-processing phase indicate that converting images to the YCbCr color space in the Cr channel is the most optimal choice for identifying areas of leaf lesions compared to other color spaces. This color space allows for an effective measurement of the number of infected pixels.

2. **Importance of Feature Selection:** The feature extraction process yields a total of 16 features, but feature selection is a crucial step in optimizing the model. The Classification Feature Selection (CFS) method produces 7 features, while Principal Component Analysis (PCA) generates 11 features. Feature selection helps narrow down the focus on truly relevant features, ultimately reducing the required computation time.

3. **Best Model Performance:** The leaf disease identification model achieves the highest accuracy of 99% when using the K-Nearest Neighbors (KNN) algorithm in combination with feature selection from PCA and CFS. This model also demonstrates excellent precision, reaching 98%, and a recall of 100%. This indicates that the model excels in recognizing healthy and infected leaves.

Overall, the use of machine learning models for identifying leaf diseases in oil palm trees has proven to be highly effective. These findings provide valuable insights into how this approach can assist in monitoring and managing the health of oil palm trees, ultimately leading to improved agricultural production and efficiency.

References

Adeel, A., Khan, M. A., Sharif, M., Azam, F., Shah, J. H., Umer, T., & Wan, S. (2019). Diagnosis and recognition of grape leaf diseases: An automated system based on a novel saliency approach and canonical correlation analysis based multiple features fusion. *Sustainable Computing: Informatics and Systems*, *24*, 100349. https://doi.org/10.1016/j.suscom.2019.08.002

Cooper, R. M., & Rusli, M. H. (2014). Threat from Fusarium wilt disease of oil palm to South-East Asia and suggested control measures. *Journal of Oil Palm Research*, *26*, 109–119.

Dey, A. K., Sharma, M., & Meshram, M. R. (2016). Image Processing Based Leaf Rot Disease, Detection of Betel Vine (Piper BetleL.). *Procedia Computer Science*, *85*(Cms), 748–754. https://doi.org/10.1016/j.procs.2016.05.262

Flood, J. (2006). A Review of Fusarium Wilt of Oil Palm Caused by Fusarium oxysporum f. sp. elaeidis. *Phytopathology®*, *96*(6), 660–662. https://doi.org/10.1094/PHYTO-96-0660

Hamdani, H., Septiarini, S., Sunyoto, A., Suyanto, S., & Utaminingrum, F. (2021). Detection of oil palm leaf disease based on color histogram and supervised classifier. *Optik*, *245*, 167753.

Husin, N. A., Khairunniza-Bejo, S., Abdullah, A. F., Kassim, M. S. M., Ahmad, D., & Aziz, M. H. A. (2020). Classification of Basal Stem Rot Disease in Oil Palm Plantations Using Terrestrial Laser Scanning Data and Machine Learning. *Agronomy*, *10*(11), 1624.

https://doi.org/10.3390/agronomy10111624

Ji, M., Zhang, L., & Wu, Q. (2020). Automatic grape leaf diseases identification via UnitedModel based on multiple convolutional neural networks. *Information Processing in Agriculture*, *7*(3), 418–426. https://doi.org/10.1016/j.inpa.2019.10.003

Jidong, L., De-An, Z., Wei, J., & Shihong, D. (2016). Recognition of apple fruit in a natural environment. *Optik*, *127*(3), 1354–1362. https://doi.org/10.1016/j.ijleo.2015.10.177

Kurihara, J., Koo, V.-C., Guey, C. W., Lee, Y. P., & Abidin, H. (2022). Early Detection of Basal Stem Rot Disease in Oil Palm Tree Using Unmanned Aerial Vehicle-Based Hyperspectral Imaging. *Remote Sensing*, *14*(3), 799. https://doi.org/10.3390/rs14030799

Masazhar, A. N. I., & Kamal, M. M. (2017). Digital image processing technique for palm oil leaf disease detection using multiclass SVM classifier. *2017 IEEE 4th International Conference on Smart Instrumentation, Measurement and Application (ICSIMA)*, *2017-Novem*(November), 1–6. https://doi.org/10.1109/ICSIMA.2017.8311978

Mattihalli, C., Gedefaye, E., Endalamaw, F., & Necho, A. (2018). Plant leaf diseases detection and auto-medicine. *Internet of Things*, *1–2*, 67–73. https://doi.org/10.1016/j.iot.2018.08.007

Md Kamal, M., Ikhwan Masazhar, A. N., & Abdul Rahman, F. (2018). Classification of Leaf Disease from Image Processing Technique. *Indonesian Journal of Electrical Engineering and Computer Science*, *10*(1), 191. https://doi.org/10.11591/ijeecs.v10.i1.pp191-200

Murphy, D. J., Goggin, K., & Paterson, R. R. M. (2021). Oil palm in the 2020s and beyond: challenges and solutions. *CABI Agriculture and Bioscience*, *2*(1), 39. https://doi.org/10.1186/s43170-021-00058-3

Pantazi, X. E., Moshou, D., & Tamouridou, A. A. (2019). Automated leaf disease detection in different crop species through image features analysis and One Class Classifiers. *Computers and Electronics in Agriculture*, *156*(November 2018), 96–104. https://doi.org/10.1016/j.compag.2018.11.005

Pornsuriya, C., Sunpapao, A., Srihanant, N., Worapattam, K., Kittimorak, J., Phithakkit, S., & Petcharat, V. (2013). A Survey of Diseases and Disorders in Oil Palms of Southern Thailand. *Plant Pathology Journal*, *12*(4), 169–175. https://doi.org/10.3923/ppj.2013.169.175

Sabzi, S., Abbaspour-Gilandeh, Y., & Javadikia, H. (2017). Machine vision system for the automatic segmentation of plants under different lighting conditions. *Biosystems Engineering*, *161*, 157–173. https://doi.org/10.1016/j.biosystemseng.2017.06.021

Sahana, M., Reshma, H., Pavithra, R., & Kavya, B. S. (2022). Plant Leaf Disease Detection Using Image Processing. In *Lecture Notes in Electrical Engineering* (Vol. 789, Nomor 1, hal. 161–168). https://doi.org/10.1007/978-981-16-1338-8_14

Saipol Anuar, M. A. S., & Syd Ali, N. (2022). Significant Oil Palm Diseases Impeding Global Industry: A Review. *Sains Malaysiana*, *51*(3), 707–721. https://doi.org/10.17576/jsm-2022-5103-06

Saleem, G., Akhtar, M., Ahmed, N., & Qureshi, W. S. (2019). Automated analysis of visual leaf shape features for plant classification. *Computers and Electronics in Agriculture, 157*(November 2018), 270–280. https://doi.org/10.1016/j.compag.2018.12.038

Santoso, H., Tani, H., & Wang, X. (2017). Random Forest classification model of basal stem rot disease caused by Ganoderma boninense in oil palm plantations. *International Journal of Remote Sensing, 38*(16), 4683–4699. https://doi.org/10.1080/01431161.2017.1331474

Septiarini, A., Hamdani, H., Hatta, H. R., & Anwar, K. (2020). Automatic image segmentation of oil palm fruits by applying the contour-based approach. *Scientia Horticulturae, 261*(June), 108939. https://doi.org/10.1016/j.scienta.2019.108939

Sethy, P. K., Barpanda, N. K., Rath, A. K., & Behera, S. K. (2020). Image Processing Techniques for Diagnosing Rice Plant Disease: A Survey. *Procedia Computer Science, 167*(2019), 516–530. https://doi.org/10.1016/j.procs.2020.03.308

Singh, V., & Misra, A. K. (2017). Detection of plant leaf diseases using image segmentation and soft computing techniques. *Information Processing in Agriculture, 4*(1), 41–49. https://doi.org/10.1016/j.inpa.2016.10.005

Suwandi, Akino, S., & Kondo, N. (2012). Common Spear Rot of Oil Palm in Indonesia. *Plant Disease, 96*(4), 537–543. https://doi.org/10.1094/PDIS-08-10-0569

Varalakshmi, P., & Aravindkumar, S. (2019). Plant disorder precognition by image based pattern recognition. *Procedia Computer Science, 165*(2019), 502–510.

About Author

Hamdani, hailing from the Department of Informatics, Faculty of Engineering at Universitas Mulawarman in East Kalimantan, Indonesia, is a distinguished figure in the realms of computer systems and technology. With a notable career dedicated to pioneering inventive solutions for real-world challenges, he has specifically delved into the domains of machine learning and image analysis. His contributions have been instrumental in the progress of disease identification in oil palm leaves, underscoring his expertise in this vital area of study.

Anindita Septiarini, also affiliated with the Department of Informatics, Faculty of Engineering at Universitas Mulawarman in East Kalimantan, Indonesia, is a fervent advocate for the integration of machine learning in agriculture and plant health. Her remarkable research endeavors within the field of disease identification in oil palm leaves have earned her well-deserved acclaim. Anindita's commitment lies in forging a seamless connection between technology and agriculture, with the ultimate goal of enhancing crop yields and fostering sustainable agricultural practices. Together, these authors bring a wealth of knowledge and passion to the subject matter, making their contributions to "Machine Learning for Disease Identification in Oil Palm Leaves" invaluable.

Emy Setyaningsih is a dedicated educator and researcher, with a strong background in the Department of Computer Systems Engineering at Institut Sains & Technology AKPRIND Yogyakarta, Indonesia. Her work in the development of machine learning models for disease identification has been instrumental in addressing the challenges faced by the agriculture industry. Emy is committed to the integration of technology for the betterment of society.

The authors, who are affiliated with the Department of Informatics, Faculty of Engineering at Universitas Mulawarman in East Kalimantan, and the Department of Computer Systems Engineering at Institut Sains & Technology AKPRIND Yogyakarta, are dedicated faculty members who continually inspire and educate the next generation of computer scientists and researchers. Through their collaborative efforts, they have produced this comprehensive manual on machine learning for the identification of diseases in oil palm leaves.